Turning Connections Into Customers

Increasing Your Internet Profits

Bonnie Dye

Turning Connections Into Customers
Increasing Your Internet Profits
Bonnie Dye

ISBN 1456319337

EAN-13 9781456319335.

Printed in the U.S.A.

Acknowledgements

To all the leaders who have shared their wisdom with me, you have shown me the way to create more personal freedom than I ever thought possible. I appreciate and honor each of you for the special gifts you share.

To Dan Stojadinovic, I'm forever grateful for the "no nonsense" approach you bring to everything you do, and I always know you'll give me a straight answer, whether or not it's what I want to hear.

To Barbara Grassey, your personal strength and courage inspires me, and I appreciate the truth you deliver with your wit. Oh yeah, and thanks for being my friend too, and putting up with my habit of chasing the newest shiny object.

To Chris Krimitsos, you've helped me see the personal gifts I bring, and for that I'm immensely grateful. Your generous spirit and dedicated work ethic has given me hope in many, many ways.

And to Kytka Hilmar-Jezek, without your tremendous skills, and your willingness to teach them, this book would never have made it from my head to the page. Thanks for your encouragement (and a swift kick now and then) that helped me make it happen.

Foreword

The idea for this book came to me as I watched fellow internet marketers scramble to embrace Social Media marketing, only to find out later that it's not really bringing them paying customers. Worse yet, as they took time away from their traditional marketing to concentrate on Facebook and Twitter, they realized their sales actually started to decline.

I soon realized that in spite of all the advantages of social media, the secret to success seems to be the same as it's always been: Everyone wants to do business with the people they know and trust. And our Social Media "friends" don't really know or trust us. Have you noticed? All of our sales are still coming from the people we talk to face to face.

There's nothing wrong with the tried and true method of having workshops... I've learned a lot from them. But what happens if you don't want to do workshops and seminars? How do you get people to know you and trust you if you don't want to travel all over the county?

Honestly, it's all about relationships. I've discovered the secret to creating great relationships online, and I'm going to tell you exactly what it is. Are you ready? The secret is to merge together traditional marketing and social media, but... and this is a big but... you have to do it in exactly the right way.

If you're an internet marketer then you've probably noticed that you can't "friend" someone and immediately get them to come to a seminar and give you money. It's just not happening.

If you're tired of spending hours on Facebook & Twitter for very little return, then this book is for you. I've included the information you've been looking for, so you too can turn your Social Media Connections into Buying Customers.

Table of Contents

Busting the Social Media Myth   1

Part 1 How and Why the Internet Money
Funnel Works   5
       What We Can Learn From Television   6
       The Psychology of the Infomercial   8
       Attraction Marketing   11

Part 2 YouTube—The In's and Outs of
Making Movies   31
       Yes, You Too Can Be a Star!   32

Part 3 Article Marketing—Why It Still Works   37
       It's Worth the Effort   38
       Creating Great Content   41
       Getting More From Your Article
       Submissions   44

Part 4 Search Engine Optimization Made Easy   47
       Choosing An Effective Domain Name   48
       The Importance of Title Tags   51
       Using Effective Keywords   55
       BackLinks   58

Part 5 Text Blog—No, It's Not An Online Diary   61
       Text Blog—The Key To Providing Good
       Content   62

Part 6 Video Blog—Creating Great Relationships   65
       Video Blog—The Key To Creating Great
       Relationships   66

Part 7 The Squeeze Page—Capturing Names
and Emails   69
    Getting Your Readers
    To Take Action   70

Part 8 The Sales Page—Creating a Page
That Gets Buyers   73
    Increase Your On-Line Success   74
    Facts Tell, Stories Sell   76
    Learn To Write Better Headlines   80
    Writing Effective Headlines   83
    Logo, Banner & Graphic Design   85
    Elements and Principles
    of Graphic Design   88

Part 9 It's Payday!   91
    Choosing the Right Merchant
    Account Provider   92
    Accepting Credit Cards Without
    a Merchant Account   96

Part 10 Customer Service Counts   99
    Creating a New Standard
    of Excellence   100
    Customer Service is Now
    Customer Care   102
    Customer Service Tips
    That Generate Referrals   104
    Delivering Great Customer Service   107

About the Author   113

Busting the Social Media Myth

Since the beginning of the Social Media boom internet gurus have been telling us how easy it is to get new customers through online connections. What they're NOT telling you is that there's a big difference between a customer and a buyer

I agree that Facebook, Twitter and others have given us a great (and cheap!) new way to collect names, but there's still no magic wand that turns these names into money in your pocket. Think about how many event invitations you get. There are a lot of internet marketers among my online friends and followers, so for me there are several new notices every day. In the past six months I've been invited to more seminars and workshops than I could attend in a decade... if I even wanted to.

Here's my point: If all of these people are making so much money from Social Media "customers," why do they keep having live events?

Even a small seminar is expensive and time consuming to produce. By the time you add up the cost of the room, some coffee and water service, and printing costs for handouts, you've already spent several hundred dollars. And that doesn't count the equipment you need. Add in a projector and microphones and you've quickly topped a thousand. For a larger event you'll need to spend many thousands.

Then there's all the time involved. Creating a pre-sentation takes days of tweaking. And if you plan to sell something at the end (and who doesn't!) you'd better put together a good bonus offer and practice, practice, practice.

Why are they doing all that if the money is pouring in from thousands of Social Media contacts? Are they really that greedy for a few extra bucks?

Maybe a few are, but many of the people I know are barely getting by. They're living from workshop to workshop, making just enough money to get through to the next one.

That's because the thousands of contacts are just that—they're initial contacts. It's a thinner connec-tion than you'll get from a speed-networking event... and that's pretty thin. You've heard the name, you've seen the face and their elevator speech sounds just like a hundred others. Pretty soon all the identities start to run together, and none of them seem worth a $99 workshop fee.

The well used adage is still true: We all want to do business with the people we know and trust. The old classmates I know and trust are the few I'm still close with. For the rest, I either barely recognize them or I remember them vividly... and not in a good way. I'm not the least bit interested in giving them my time or my money just because we grew up in the same community—at least not right away.

And that's why I've written this book. I've discovered a way to turn those initial contacts into buyers. And you can do it too, without sponsoring a live event or spending a lot of money for ads. I call it the Internet Money Funnel and it works for any kind of business. Whether you have a physical product or a digital download, when you put it into the funnel, money from buyers will pour out the other end.

You see, it's all about creating relationships. I'm going to show you how to create real relationships with the people you come in contact with. You'll be able to let your followers know you and trust you in a way that makes them willing—and ready—to do business with you.

Part 1

How and Why the Internet Money Funnel Works

What We Can Learn From Television

TVLand and Nick-at-Night aren't the only places we find classic television shows. They're cropping up everywhere, more and more. There are websites and online stores whose sole purpose is to sell classic television paraphernalia. These sites are capitalizing on the baby boomer's affinity for nostalgia.

Donny and Marie, Sonny and Cher, The Partridge Family, The Walton's, The Brady Bunch, Superman, The Flintstones, Scooby Doo, and even the Dukes of Hazzard are popping up all over the place.

The appeal of these shows for many isn't the acting or the story line. The true value is in the nostalgia. You can't put a price on the memories or the feelings that are released when you revisit the good old days of your favorite shows.

These feelings come from the relationships we had with the characters in the show. We knew their likes and dislikes as well as their strengths and weak-nesses, and we watched each week to see how they would work through their latest problem.

If anyone had tried to tell me as a teenager that I cared about those people, I'd have brushed it off with a comment like, "I just want to see what hap-pens each week." I didn't realize then that "wanting to see what happens" comes from caring about the personality on the screen.

Nowadays, we have a unique ability to let other people see our personalities, even if they've never met us. Through the use of Social Media, Video, Webinars and Conferencing, you can let your online friends and followers get to know you from the comfort of their own home (or favorite coffee shop).

If you want to take full advantage of the thousands of contacts available to you through your online connections, you must be willing to spend a little time letting them get to know and trust you. This can be done with a minimum amount of effort. It's much, much easier than traveling all over the country doing workshops and presentations. Not to mention all the money you'll save.

The Psychology of the Infomercial

Internet Marketing specialists can learn a great deal from infomercials. There's a lot of similarity between them and a typical sales letter. As we continue to have access to new kinds of easy video sharing, it no longer needs to cost tens of thousands of dollars to get yourself or your product seen.

Many companies (large and small) are finding it hard to maintain profits during the current economic recession, but infomercials are flourishing. One major reason for this is that people are putting off the trip to the mall, and instead are spending more time at home. It's safer, they think, to avoid being tempted by window shopping. And since they can skip past the commercials on TV, they feel like they're taking good care of their budget.

The actual result, however, is quite the opposite. More time at home means more time in front of the television. And even though we zoom past routine ads, an "information commercial" often looks like a regular program. A well planned infomercial sounds mildly educational... more like entertainment than advertising... and our mind is quickly fooled into relaxing, with no resistance to the sales pitch that's inevitably on its way.

Another major factor is that most of the "As Seen on TV" products are not made by a major corporation, so there's no brand awareness. This again acts to remove any fear we might have about being sold to. The promoter is seen as just a regular guy who's very excited to show you the cool new gadget you can have.

In short, an infomercial is a direct response ad just like many you may have seen (or created) on the internet. It's just a call to action.

For years we've been trying to copy this process in our sales letters, with mediocre results. We use all the same concepts, including Bonuses, "Buy Now" price reductions, and pop-ups that urge us not to leave ("But wait—there's more!").

So why doesn't it work as well for us as it does on TV? The answer is as plain as the writing on your monitor. And I mean that literally. There's only a certain amount of emotion you can convey with text. After a while we get numb to the headlines, bullet points and other attention getting ploys, and it all starts to look like minor variations of plain text.

Psychological studies have shown that infomercials are more successful because we are partially influenced by the facial expressions of the spokesperson. You can probably see where I'm going with this. You need to be turning your networking connections into real relationships. And to do that profitably, you need to be using video.

I'll be discussing this more in the Sales Page chapter, but I want to mention another important aspect of the television pitch. Their sales tactic is obvious, and it's the same every time, and yet we still really love seeing the product price dropping while the pile of stuff you'll get keeps increasing. Take a clue from these experts and add more bonuses AFTER you've lowered the price. Every internet guru I've seen lists all the bonuses before the price is finally revealed. It's like giving the punch line too soon. How could we have missed this for so long?

Attraction Marketing

What is Attraction Marketing?

We're all familiar with the popular pay per click advertisements that many online business owners use. It's a very effective tool for driving traffic to your website, but the real question is, "what will your visitors experience once they get to your site?"

In today's internet, (often called Web 2.0) your marketing campaigns should be designed to pull, not push, customers to your website through a process known as attraction marketing. Web 2.0 is all about interacting with others. By engaging your audience with relevant content they can actually experience, you give them a reason to stay on your site longer once they're there—and a reason to come back. Online gaming, message boards, short videos, mobile content, email and SMS are just a few examples of this type of attraction (or interactive) marketing.

Be Relevant to Your Market

For clients to be attracted to you, it's important for you to know your customer base and design your interactions to fit their needs. If you sell Metamucil to a target audience that's over fifty, online gaming and SMS are probably not your best advertising bets. On the other hand, if your niche market is teens and 'tweens, those could both be very enticing avenues. There are basically three keys to attraction marketing:

relevance, relevance, and relevance. The following are just some practical examples of using interactions to connect with your audience.

- If you send out an e-newsletter, give your customers a reason to read it—don't just tell them what you're selling. Talk about something they'll care about. If you sell shot glasses, your customers would probably like to know how to play the new drinking game you learned over the holidays. And while they're reading, they'll just happen to see the new products you're offering as well.

- Get creative. Find some popular blogs that pertain to what you're selling and send them samples. Ask them to review it on their blogs.

- With mobile content, you're sending interesting and relevant messages to opt-in customers' mobile phones and saying, "Hey, we brought this to you." The Mobile Marketing Association (mma-Global.com) can provide you with information on the way mobile content is being used as well as resources for getting set up if you choose to use that option in your advertising campaign.

Branding
Branding is a lot more than a company and a logo... it's a relationship between the brand and the audience. Attraction marketing can really give you a leg up on making that connection with your audience

and engaging them with interaction. That's how you differentiate yourself from every other web store out there. The goal is for your brand to become a part of your customers' lives—you're on their phones, their computers and in their inboxes. When they think of the type of goods you sell, they think of you!

In this new frontier of Social Media marketing, you can spike your traffic fast, and if you do it right, you'll get long term search engine traffic too. It's really the best of both worlds. Free traffic and higher search engine rankings!

Plus! Higher Conversions

Here's the final key ingredient... and that's the fact that social media marketing means that the huge flood of extra traffic you'll get to your site is already PRE-SOLD. You already have a relationship with them... and they are going to convert into customers at a rate you haven't seen since your grandmother visited your lemonade stand when you were a kid.

It's this simple... people like to buy from people they already know, like, and trust. By using attraction marketing through social media, you will have the kind of presence that allows people to already know you, like you, and trust you before they even hit your web site. It's that simple.

A recent test was performed by a well respected marketing analysis firm, MarketingExperiments.com.

The company runs online tests and records the results in their newsletters. They recently concluded a 12-month test for a series of 4 websites. The analysts measured the results of social media marketing versus buying paid traffic.

Here is what they found...

Using social media marketing they were able to generate over 93,000 visitors to their sites over the full testing period, for an average of 7750 visitors per month. During that time they paid an employee a total of $3600 to do the social media marketing work, resulting in a total cost per visitor of 4 cents.

Next they ran a one month test to drive traffic from Google AdWords. Using that strategy they obtained 2,057 visitors after investing $1,250 in click costs, resulting in a cost per visitor of 61 cents. By comparison, 4 cents versus 61 cents—social media marketing yielded a 1,427% better return on their investment. Not bad!

Whether you're using Facebook, Twitter or another social media platform, it's all about creating a presence on each one, adding friends and followers, then developing a relationship with each of them. The rest (traffic) comes naturally when you use social media to create attraction marketing the right way!

Most business owners do not effectively attract and retain lifetime customers. This happens because they don't understand the key principles of relationship marketing, and what behaviors convert potential customers into repeat clients.

To succeed in your business, your main goal should be to build a responsive email list of lifetime customers from your targeted market. It's your job to make sure these people learn to trust you, feel grateful to you and value your recommendation.

A good relationship with loyal customers is worth a fortune. It's the most valuable asset any business can have. Achieve this and you're set for life.

For that reason you need to learn the key principles of relationship marketing to be able to apply attraction marketing concepts to your web site.

What Is Relationship Marketing?
Relationship marketing is the method of gradually turning website visitors into subscribers. The process leads them from position to position along a planned program to convert them into lifetime customers.

Think of relationship building as the foundation to your business. It establishes you as a trustworthy professional and a consistent source.

Admittedly it's more difficult to build a relationship

online than offline, even though the technique for each is almost the same. Turning an offline customer into a lifetime customer is easier because of the face to face connection you already have. Obviously, in online marketing you can't meet most of your clients in person. You can, however, build these connections into relationships if you always think first about what you can give to your potential clients, rather than what you will get from them. This thought process is important throughout each step you take when building your business. Attraction marketing through relationship building is a process, not just a one-time commitment. It starts the moment you think about building a business and continues as long as you stay in.

Know Your Potential Customers

Before you start building your business you need to determine your target market and know the likes and dislikes of your potential customers. By learning as much as possible about your customers you can develop effective tactics for delivering your message to them.

You can start getting to know your customers by taking some very simple steps.

- Determine in advance where your potential customers congregate.

- What newsletters do they read?

- What forums do they visit and post to?

- What else might they do while surfing the net?

The best places to find your prospects are forums, discussion groups and discussion boards. Relationships are not only based on knowing who your visitors are, but on knowing your customers' and prospects' specific needs. By visiting forums which are of interest to your targeted market you can determine several key factors.

What problems do your potential customers have in common?

- What are they are looking for?

- What kind of businesses are they are involved in?

- How do they want their problem to be solved?

- What words do they use?

To attract more subscribers and build a strong attraction marketing campaign the easy way, use the words your prospects are likely to use. If you feel their pain and use their words when posting to forums and sending messages, they'll be able to relate to you. You will be one of them. You will not seem like a stranger and they will be likely to trust you and consider your recommendation.

Show Your Expertise

The majority of business people never completely and clearly display their knowledge to potential customers. Show your targeted market that you are the leader in your industry and they will follow you.

People like to learn about your experience. They like to follow the expert's steps to avoid mistakes and reach success the easy way with less investment in time and money.

Start a Dialog To Establish Trust

Setting up a continuing dialog will establish trust. This is a vital step to building long-time relationships, and it is especially easy today with the popularity of social media. The dialog with your new prospect should start as soon as your visitor and you have made an initial connection.

Your goal is to create long term relationships which will turn your contacts into subscribers. To do that you must invest time to gather available sources and high quality information and put it at your prospects' disposal to help them succeed. Remember, maintaining customer enthusiasm and creating customer loyalty is your key to success.

Follow Up

Dialog leads to follow-up. Engage your subscribers with comments about things that are happening in your personal life as well as your business. It's important to share some personal information now and then to make you seem like a real person your prospects can relate to. Keep in mind though, it's important to avoid controversial subjects unless the topic is specifically related to your product or service. Professionalism is the key to building successful relationships.

The main purpose of follow up is to remain visible to your subscribers so, when the need arises and your prospect wants to make a purchase, your product will be the first one the subscriber thinks of.

If you want to have lifelong commitments from your customers, you must not stop giving them attention when they have purchased your product. Going after one sale is worthless. Your marketing tactic should include following up with your customer after the sale is made. This important step will help you strengthen the relationship and decrease the potential for refund requests. It will also keep your customer buying from you again and again.

Your follow-up should continue long after the first purchase. Share information other than just sales messages. From time to time send free useful products they can't easily find elsewhere—make it something that can help them make money and/or save time. For your loyal repeat customers, send special offers with discounts that are available for those loyal customers only. Keep them up to date and to the point with the latest product news, etc...

Offer Good Customer Service

Some people will start an online business and only focus on what services or products they can sell. They are not worried about establishing good relationships with their customers and potential clients. This attitude will doom your business to failure. Good customer service doesn't need to be difficult. There are some business habits that are key to providing good service. If you put these ideas in place before you have a problem, you can avoid having a small issue turn into a big one.

- Answer your prospects' requests as soon as you receive them.

- Reply to every email within 24 hours with the needed response whether it is a question, concern or simply someone looking for more information.

- Treat your customers like you would expect to be treated. Even if you offer the best products or services, most customers will evaluate your business by how they were treated while doing business with you.

By providing great customer service to the people you do business with, you will get customers coming back to you again and again to buy your products or services.

Another aspect of good customer service is to ask for their feedback. Only by knowing your customers' wants and needs can you successfully grow your business. Attraction marketing requires you to be totally customer-oriented.

Having a contact page on your website with a comment or feedback form will keep you informed about your customers' wants and problems. If you publish a newsletter, you can also accomplish this by asking for feedback from your subscribers. This is a great way to let your audience know you care about what they have to say and how important they are to you. When you show interest in your customers you will build credibility and loyalty.

Educate Your Subscribers

Make it easy for your customers to find manuals for your product, a frequently asked question (FAQ) web page, articles, etc... to help them learn how to use your product or service perfectly. Educate your subscribers to help them build interest and loyalty for your business.

Lifetime clients want you to be their trusted advisor. The more you educate your customers by offering them a variety of options, the greater your chance to earn their lifetime business. Education strengthens relationship marketing with clients.

Sell Or Recommend Only Quality Products

Sell quality products that have value, plus offer a guarantee and stand behind it. One of the quickest ways to destroy a business relationship is selling poor quality products and not standing behind what you promise.

If you want to promote other marketers' affiliate programs from your website, take the time to investigate the companies you advocate. Promote only products from legitimate companies with solid internet presence. Remember, the companies you suggest will have an impact on your business reputation.

Relationship building is the cornerstone of attraction marketing. If you follow these key principles you'll be on your way to building a responsive opt in email list which will lead to more and better sales.

A good relationship with loyal customers is worth a fortune. It's the most valuable asset any business can have. Achieve this and you're set for life.

For that reason you need to learn the key principles of relationship marketing to be able to apply attraction marketing concepts to your web site.

What Is Relationship Marketing?

Relationship marketing is the method of gradually turning website visitors into subscribers. The process leads them from position to position along a planned program to convert them into lifetime customers.

Think of relationship building as the foundation to

your business. It establishes you as a trustworthy professional and a consistent source.

Admittedly it's more difficult to build a relationship online than offline, even though the technique for each is almost the same. Turning an offline customer into a lifetime customer is easier because of the face to face connection you already have. Obviously, in online marketing you can't meet most of your clients in person. You can, however, build these connections into relationships if you always think first about what you can give to your potential clients, rather than what you will get from them. This thought process is important throughout each step you take when building your business. Attraction marketing through relationship building is a process, not just a one-time commitment. It starts the moment you think about building a business and continues as long as you stay in.

Know Your Potential Customers
Before you start building your business you need to determine your target market and know the likes and dislikes of your potential customers. By learning as much as possible about your customers you can develop effective tactics for delivering your message to them.

You can start getting to know your customers by taking some very simple steps.

- Determine in advance where your potential customers congregate.

- What newsletters do they read?

- What forums do they visit and post to?

- What else might they do while surfing the net?

The best places to find your prospects are forums, discussion groups and discussion boards. Relationships are not only based on knowing who your visitors are, but on knowing your customers' and prospects' specific needs. By visiting forums which are of interest to your targeted market you can determine several key factors.

- What problems do your potential customers have in common?

- What are they are looking for?

- What kind of businesses are they are involved in?

- How do they want their problem to be solved?

- What words do they use?

To attract more subscribers and build a strong attraction marketing campaign the easy way, use the words your prospects are likely to use. If you feel their pain and use their words when posting to forums and sending messages, they'll be able to relate to you. You will be one of them. You will not seem like a stranger and they will be likely to trust you and consider your recommendation.

Show Your Expertise

The majority of business people never completely and clearly display their knowledge to potential customers. Show your targeted market that you are the leader in your industry and they will follow you.

People like to learn about your experience. They like to follow the expert's steps to avoid mistakes and reach success the easy way with less investment in time and money.

Start a Dialog To Establish Trust

Setting up a continuing dialog will establish trust. This is a vital step to building long-time relationships, and it is especially easy today with the popularity of social media. The dialog with your new prospect should start as soon as your visitor and you have made an initial connection.

Your goal is to create long term relationships which will turn your contacts into subscribers. To do that you must invest time to gather available sources and high quality information and put it at your prospects' disposal to help them succeed. Remember, maintaining customer enthusiasm and creating customer loyalty is your key to success.

Follow Up

Dialog leads to follow-up. Engage your subscribers with comments about things that are happening in your personal life as well as your business. It's important to share some personal information now and then to make you seem like a real person your prospects can relate to. Keep in mind though, it's important to avoid controversial subjects unless the topic is specifically related to your product or service. Professionalism is the key to building successful relationships.

The main purpose of follow up is to remain visible to your subscribers so, when the need arises and your prospect wants to make a purchase, your product will be the first one the subscriber thinks of.

If you want to have lifelong commitments from your customers, you must not stop giving them attention when they have purchased your product. Going after one sale is worthless. Your marketing tactic should include following up with your customer after the sale is made. This important step will help you strengthen the relationship and decrease the potential for refund requests. It will also keep your customer buying from you again and again.

Your follow-up should continue long after the first purchase. Share information other than just sales messages. From time to time send free useful products they can't easily find elsewhere—make it something that can help them make money and/or save time. For your loyal repeat customers, send special offers with discounts that are available for those loyal customers only. Keep them up to date and to the point with the latest product news, etc...

Offer Good Customer Service

Some people will start an online business and only focus on what services or products they can sell. They are not worried about establishing good relationships with their customers and potential clients. This attitude will doom your business to failure. Good customer service doesn't need to be difficult. There are some business habits that are key to providing good service. If you put these ideas in place before you have a problem, you can avoid having a small issue turn into a big one.

- Answer your prospects' requests as soon as you receive them.

- Reply to every email within 24 hours with the needed response whether it is a question, concern or simply someone looking for more information.

- Treat your customers like you would expect to be treated. Even if you offer the best products or services, most customers will evaluate your business by how they were treated while doing business with you.

By providing great customer service to the people you do business with, you will get customers coming back to you again and again to buy your products or services.

Another aspect of good customer service is to ask for their feedback. Only by knowing your customers' wants and needs can you successfully grow your business. Attraction marketing requires you to be totally customer-oriented.

Having a contact page on your website with a comment or feedback form will keep you informed about your customers' wants and problems. If you publish a newsletter, you can also accomplish this by asking for feedback from your subscribers. This is a great way to let your audience know you care about what they have to say and how important they are to you. When you show interest in your customers you will build credibility and loyalty.

Educate Your Subscribers

Make it easy for your customers to find manuals for your product, a frequently asked question (FAQ) web page, articles, etc... to help them learn how to use your product or service perfectly. Educate your subscribers to help them build interest and loyalty for your business.

Lifetime clients want you to be their trusted advisor. The more you educate your customers by offering them a variety of options, the greater your chance to earn their lifetime business. Education strengthens relationship marketing with clients.

Sell or Recommend Only Quality Products

Sell quality products that have value, plus offer a guarantee and stand behind it. One of the quickest ways to destroy a business relationship is selling poor quality products and not standing behind what you promise.

If you want to promote other marketers' affiliate programs from your website, take the time to investigate the companies you advocate. Promote only products from legitimate companies with solid internet presence. Remember, the companies you suggest will have an impact on your business reputation.

Relationship building is the cornerstone of attraction marketing. If you follow these key principles you'll be on your way to building a responsive opt in email list which will lead to more and better sales.

Part 2

YouTube

—

The In's and Outs of Making Movies

Yes, You Too Can Be a Star!

There was a time when the internet was only used for research. As the popularity of the internet grew, so did the way it was used. Today billions of people rely on the internet for entertainment, and YouTube has become one of the largest entertainment databases in the world. In fact, it is so popular that when asked about video sites many individuals automatically respond with YouTube.

The online video website allows you to view homemade videos and tutorials, and you can also make and share your own productions. The vast majority of the videos found on YouTube have been created by everyday people just like you and me. The videos are streamed, which allows them to load and play quickly.

A large number of internet users of all ages are making the decision to make their own videos. Many of these videos are used to share information with others, showcase a favorite scene from one of their favorite television shows, express their beliefs, or just to create comedy. This is something that is literally amazing. Millions of individuals have a good idea or some thoughts they would like to document or share, but many would be unable to do so without the assistance of YouTube. After you have created your own video, you can easily have it uploaded, often in as little as a few minutes.

In spite of it's popularity, many people are still shy when it comes to making online videos. This does not necessarily involve the video content, but is more often about the technical process of how the video will be made and uploaded to the system. If you are planning to make a video for YouTube, you can relax and worry about other things. The uploading process they use is probably one of the easiest you'll find online.

Of course, the first step will be to make your video. To do this, you just need a standard video recording device. These devices most commonly include camcorders and webcams. You can make just about any type of video you want, however it's important to remember that your video will be seen by thousands or even millions of internet users. For this reason, make sure your video content is appropriate. If you plan to include any graphic materials or foul language, it's a good idea to make note of it in the video's title.

When making your video, it's also important to note that YouTube has a number of limitations. Those limitations include the length of your video and the size of your video's file. YouTube currently requires that your video be no more than ten minutes in length. It is also required that your videos be less than 2GB in size. However, aside from their other rules, stipulated in their Terms of Use agreement, there are no other restrictions. This means that you can create as many videos as you want. In fact, if you would like to make a video that is longer than ten minutes, you can do so by making it a two part video.

To upload your movie to YouTube you must be able to save your video using a movie making software program. There are a number of different programs you can use, with the two most common being MovieMaker and IMovie. These programs can easily be obtained, but most newer computers already have one of these programs installed. Once you load a video onto your computer, the program enables you to edit and save your video. Of course, editing is not required, and many people prefer to see an unedited version.

Before you can upload a video to YouTube, you must register for a free membership. The free membership is undoubtedly one of the reasons YouTube has remained so popular. There are a fairly large number of online video sites and each one operates in a slightly different way. Some online sites charge you to become a member and others charge you to watch certain videos. According to their website, YouTube is completely free. Not only can you watch videos made by others, but you can also make your own and have access to a number of different YouTube features, without having to pay a thing.

The signup process is just used to attach your information to your videos and keep track of all of them, especially if you decide to upload more than one. Once you've signed up you'll see an option that will allow you to create or upload your own videos. Simply follow the onscreen directions. Depending on the type of internet connection your have, your videos could be uploaded and ready for viewing in as little as a few minutes.

From their home page at YouTube.com you can immediately begin searching for videos to watch, even if you choose not to register. It's easy to find something you want to watch on YouTube. With a simple keyword search you'll be provided with videos matching your criteria. In addition to performing a standard search, you're also be able to browse through the videos that are hosted on the site. You can browse through videos by highest rankings, most comments, most views, and most linked. All of these videos are ones that have most likely generated the most internet buzz.

While YouTube is a great place to watch all different kinds of videos, it's important to keep one thing in mind. YouTube is used by a large number of internet users. In fact, it can easily be considered the most popular online video website. This means that different individuals with different views and beliefs will be posting homemade videos. YouTube does regulate the videos that are hosted on their site, but it is possible that you may be offended by some of the videos you see. Although it is difficult to determine what a video's content will be by the video title, you are advised to avoid videos with titles may that cause you some concern.

In addition to being free, YouTube is also popular because it is easy to use. You do not have to be an experienced internet user to enjoy this online enter- tainment. With easy to use categories and search features, you should be able to find and watch online videos that peak your interest, without having to spend hours or even days familiarizing yourself with the website.

Part 3

Article Marketing

—

Why It Still Works

It's Worth the Effort

Looking for a simple way to get an edge on your competition?

Successful businesses who are in it for the long haul continually apply innovative marketing strategies and tactics to differentiate themselves and get that edge. Two such killer marketing strategies are positioning and relationship building. And guess what? Article marketing is a proven tactic that just happens to address both of those marketing strategies. Is it the "be all, end all" of positioning and relationship building? Absolutely not. However, it is an excellent step in the right direction. And on top of that, there's probably a good chance that your competition is not using this tactic. Face it. It takes some time, skill, and effort to write and effectively use articles. That's why the masses don't do it. However, those looking for an edge do.

So why choose article marketing as one of your marketing tactics? Here are some exceptional reasons:

It is quite simple. People love to buy from and deal with the best. Writing and effectively marketing your articles helps you position yourself as the expert in your field.

Let's take this first concept a step further for reason #2. Let's be blunt here. As an expert, you can justifiably increase your rates and charge more for your products.

If your articles are good and distributed properly, they can spread like wildfire and literally cause a viral marketing frenzy. This will ultimately drive business your way.

A big part of Internet marketing has to do with the Search Engines like Google, Yahoo, Bing, etc. It's critical that we play their game. That being said, Search Engines love content such as articles. Many Internet marketers try the latest fad to trick Search Engines into getting a better ranking. If you have a lot of time and/or money on your hands to keep up with the latest trends and the ever changing Search Engine rules, then you can chase the latest shiny object. However, one tactic still holds true with improving Search Engine ranking, and that's article marketing.

People love to feel well informed—it helps them make better decisions. Your articles can serve as the source for the input they seek. And who better to buy from than the source that provided the information in the first place!

Talk about getting major bang for the buck, articles can easily be repurposed in a variety of ways. For example:

- They can become content for your newsletter

- Used as free giveaways to prospects/clients, in seminars, at networking events, etc

- Used to spark conversation in a blog or an online networking group

- Combine multiple articles into an eBook, book or info-product that can be sold or given away in exchange for contact information

- Become the basis for a live seminar or webinar

- And we can go on and on and on!

Articles, when distributed properly are a great way to stay in touch with clients and prospects. Studies have shown that on average it takes 7 touches before a prospect buys. Why not use articles as some of those touches? This will help continually boost your prospect's perception of you as someone who consistently adds value.

We live in an age where information is king. We all know something others would be interested in knowing. Share your knowledge and like a magnet, you'll attract your prospects to you.

Creating Great Content

We've all heard it... "Content is King", and for good reason. Web surfers come online for two reasons: 1) to check email or social sites, and 2) to search for information. That's why, in the early days of the Internet, it was called the "Information Super-Highway". An article is an excellent source of information, and you can be the one who supplies it.

There are countless reasons to use Article Marketing as one of your online strategies, and here are just a few:

Search Engines LOVE Them

It's no secret that Search Engines LOVE content, so if you supply it on a regular basis you're giving them a great reason to stop by and take a look around. Once the search engine bot finds your article, the resource box is used to index your website and create a spider web of links to it. This is exactly what you want in your quest to create an internet presence.

Website, Blog and Newsletter Owners Always Need Them

Website owners and bloggers always need fresh content to keep their visitors and/or subscribers coming back. Newsletter publishers also need fresh content for the email newsletters which are sent to their subscriber base. Your resource box stays with your article, and each time someone else shares it, a new link is created back to you.

They Generate Lifelong Residual Traffic

Articles produce lifelong residual traffic because website owners, newsletter publishers and article directories archive them for their visitors to read and search through. I have articles that I wrote several years ago that continue to bring me new website visitors every week.

Get One-Way Links for High Page Ranking

One of the best reasons to use Article Marketing is because it helps you achieve one-way links to high ranking pages. When you offer your free information with 'Reprint Rights' and the website owner decides to archive your article within their article directory, you receive the benefit of that website's popularity. You'll be able to piggyback off their page rank rating, which gives your own website a page rank boost.

Syndicate Through RSS

You can become a "syndicated columnist". By using an RSS feed (which stands for Real Simple Syndication), website surfers can opt-in to have your next article sent directly to them. As soon as you publish something new, they are notified immediately. You can also submit your RSS feeds to search engines and directories.

Post Them To Related Forums and Newsgroups

The Internet is all about numbers, and Forums and Newsgroups contain yet another avenue for you to gain some extra exposure (for free) for your online business through your articles. Just make sure you read the Terms of Use before you start posting to an online group. Otherwise, you can be reprimanded by the group organizer for breaking the rules. (They can be Nasty.)

Get Instant Credibility

As a published author you gain instant credibility as an Expert. The best way to gain the trust of your potential customers online is to supply them with quality information. This let's your reader know that you are knowledgeable about your industry. It also creates an additional relationship connection between you and your customer.

And just think... you'll get all those benefits by producing just one article. The more you produce, the more you'll benefit. The power of Article Marketing can take your online business to the next level, and turn your initial connections into buying customers.

Getting More From Your Article Submissions

Article Submission is a great way to get traffic to your site, but in some cases articles are wasted in a directory that isn't well organized. In addition, many large directories have so many articles on so many topics that a potential reader gets overwhelmed just looking. Often the reader will leave the site to look for something else. If you submit your articles to large directories with thousands of other articles about every topic, there's less chance that your article will be viewed.

The key to making your article submissions more worthwhile is to submit to specialized directories.

You might think these specific directories are not as good because they don't get as much traffic, and it's true, their visitor count might be lower. The benefit, however, is that they are getting as much (or more!) traffic that is targeted to your specific niche. Because of this, you'll know that every person who goes to that directory is looking for an article like yours. Broad article directories are great, but I only use them when I cannot find a directory for the specific topic of my article.

The idea of submitting articles to specific article directories is compelling. This is a way to get your articles published in a place where every single person is looking for an article similar to yours. This significantly increases the chance that your article will be re-published by another website owner.

I saw an example of such a directory when I was looking for articles to fill a site about "fishing". What I found was amazing! The site had many features that a regular information/shopping site would have, but they also had an additional area where you could submit articles for others to republish. The site had a lot of good quality, useable information, and in no time you could have built a 50-page website. These high content sites can be indexed within a day, and I've seen sites like this spidered by Google within a month of publication.

These article directories are not easy to find when you type "article directories" into a search engine because they often use different key words. This is a problem because it's hard to know what key words will be found by inputting a key word into a search engine.

Yahoo is actually better than Google for this, simply because of the way Yahoo is structured. To find the directory you want you'll have to type in a more specific search phrase. For example, if you're look-ing for articles about fishing, type in, "fishing article directory". This will locate some websites related to fishing, as well as directories which are packed with articles on the topic.

Another advantage to submitting your articles to
these directories is that your site will get many back
links. In addition, you will more quickly gain a reputation for being an expert in your field. If you send
your niche articles to a directory with a broad range
of categories, sub-categories and sub-sub-categories,
you'll have a lot of trouble competing with the
professional writers. When you find a specified
directory with articles focusing on a certain topic,
you have a better chance to get you articles published all over the internet, faster than you can
imagine.

Part 4

Search Engine Optimization Made Easy

Choosing An Effective Domain Name

In the physical world, you can distinguish a business because of its structure, window displays, or signs. You can tell that a bank is a bank, or a clothing store is indeed a clothing store.

On the Internet, however, it's an entirely different story. Your domain name is the only clue to your online business. You do not have visual clues: no location, no look, and no store design. Instead, users have to type in a word or a set of words to reach your site. Your prospective visitor has no way of knowing what your site is all about until he/she finds it and reads its content. Who could ever know that Amazon.com sells books? Or that Excite is a search engine?

Your domain name can spell your success on the Internet, and a good domain name is the best asset you can have. It can make your business stand out in the crowd, or just float aimlessly in space.

The need to provide immediate clues to an online business led to the prevalence of generic domain names. Generic names instantly provide the reader with an idea of what your business is about, what to expect and what to look for on your site. For instance, it's easy to guess that Etoys.com is a toy store.

The temptation of the generic name has been so powerful that some companies even paid ridiculously high prices to get the name they want. Domain names such as Loans.com and Wines.com were purchased by large corporations for $3 million each. Telephone.com was acquired for $1.75 million, while Bingo.com sold for $1.1 million.

However, generic names do not necessarily create the "buzz" that you'd like to have surrounding your website. Branding has always been about proper names. McDonald's did not name their store Hamburger. Hertz is not called Car Rental. FedEx is not named Mail Carrier, and Kodak is not called Photographs.

For better branding results, your domain name should be memorable and easy to remember. Remember the following tips when creating a domain name.

- The domain name should be short

- The domain name should be simple

- It should be suggestive of your business category

- It should be unique

- It should be easy to interpret and pronounce

- It should be personalized

- It should not be difficult to spell

- It should not be difficult to remember

In addition, your domain name should include your best keywords. For example, if your best keyword phrase is "satellite affiliate", you'll want to choose a domain name that includes this phrase. You might therefore choose a domain such as *SatelliteAffiliateTips.com*.

Domain names can be registered through many different companies (known as 'registrars')—a listing of these companies is available at ICANN: *http://www.icann.org*. You can register for 1 to 10 years, and prices can vary anywhere from $10 to $20 per year.

Most web hosting companies will handle the registration process for you, but make sure you are properly listed as the owner of the domain when it is registered. If you have registered a domain name for a specific period, make sure you renew it in time. You'd be surprised at the number of cases in which a site owner has let a good domain name slip away because they have not renewed in time.

The Importance of Title Tags

If you are new to search engine optimization and want to boost traffic to your web site, writing good Title Tags is a great place to start.

Many web sites lack a good page title. This is often completely ignored during the design process or just poorly written. This causes two main problems: 1) A poorly written title won't get many clicks and 2) the website will be lower in the search engine rankings.

Here's what happens ...

When someone performs a search, they are provided with a list of results to choose from. This list uses your page title to display your website listing to the person doing the search. If your page title doesn't grab attention, the searcher won't click on it.

It's like writing a great book on how to catch fish, but giving it a crumby title like "A Fishing Book." It will easily get passed up in favor of the book next to it titled, "How To Catch a Lot of Fish—Easily"

Search engine rankings are determined in much the same way. Generally speaking, if your page titles don't contain keywords that people are searching for, then your pages will have a lower ranking than if your title did have those keywords.

It's important to write good titles for your website page to both increase your rankings and to attract people to click to your site.

Where To Find the Page Title

It can be found in the html source code, toward the top of the page. Don't worry, you don't have to understand how to read html, just look for the word Title. It will have a few words after it, then the word "Title" again.

How To Write a Good Title Tag

The two biggest things to keep in mind when writing your titles are:

1. Include your keywords in your title. Search engines use the words in the title tag to identify what your web page is about. Including your keywords in the title tag will improve its ranking in search engines.

2. Make your title attention-grabbing. As mentioned before, search engines use page titles when displaying results. If you make it attention-grabbing it can win more clicks and bring more traffic to your site.

Here's more advice on writing attractive, keyword rich title tags:

- Include your keywords towards the beginning of the title. This gives those keywords more prominence.

- Avoid filler-words. Words like "the," "a," and "and" just take up space and don't help your ranking.

- Use your name, your patented coaching process, book title or other well-known trademark in the title tags of the pages in which they are mentioned.

- Don't put "John Smith—Business Coach." This won't grab attention as much as something like "Business Coach—Grow your business 200%."

- Use about eight words. This is the amount that is visible in search engine result pages.

- Write titles that draw attention. Some techniques include: using keywords that people are searching on, using problem statements, benefit statements.

- Be sure your titles accurately reflect what is on the page. Misleading titles disappoint users and search engines may penalize your site.

- Don't overstuff your page title with keywords. It creates a bad looking title in search listings and puts your page at risk for search engine penalties.

- Don't keep the same title tag across multiple pages. This implies the pages are of the same content and they really aren't. This is seen as a minus in the eyes of search engines.

Here's an example of a title tag for the home page of a career coach web site:

"Career Coach for Accountants and Lawyers—Increase Your Earnings"

You can see that this title includes a benefit statement, relevant keywords, and the target audience's name—good for rankings and good for getting attention.

Both from an SEO perspective and from an overall marketing perspective, the most effective title is one that offers an accurate description of the page, yet short enough to display completely in the search engine results pages. In most cases, 60 characters or less will be adequate to describe a web page and still display completely in most search engines.

Using Effective Keywords

For Search Engine Optimization, keywords are of supreme importance. Because these are words or phrases that search engines use in order to match web pages with search queries, it's important to optimize your website with strategic keywords in order to maximize targeted traffic. You will use keywords in both your on-page and off-page optimization.

Know what words your customers will use when searching. You might already know what your customers are searching for, but if not, it's important for you to find out. For example, if you have a website that sells clothing, you could use a description of "pants" or "jeans." One may be searched more often than the other, but why not target both? How about a website selling "executive gifts?" Maybe "desk accessories" will broaden your website marketing strategy.

One of the best tools to use when deciding on keywords is Google Keyword Tool. It's free, and comes with a great collection of tutorials. To find it, just go to Google Search and type in Keyword Tool.

Once you have successfully harvested a meaningful keyword list, remove any keywords that are too targeted or not specific enough. Also remember that keyword placement is important. Try to put as many keywords as possible in the beginning paragraphs, and also in the title line.

In addition, the keywords should appear regularly throughout the opening Web page. It is especially important that they appear frequently in the opening paragraphs. Scatter keywords throughout the content of your page to a keyword density of between 3%-7%, and resist the temptation to overuse keywords. Using a keyword too frequently can trigger a search engine's "keyword stuffing" filter. The search engines use such a filter in an effort to prevent search engine spam from appearing in the top results. The search engines can spot it and will reduce your page rankings if you do this.

Tools are available to help with optimal keyword density. However, avoid software that automatically writes the site's pages. The search engines can sniff these out, too. A good rule of thumb is: Never sacrifice quality of content for keyword placement. This will affect your page ranking. More importantly, your site won't appeal to visitors.

It's also helpful to add common misspellings of a word as well as both the singular and plural forms of the word or phrase.

Use your keywords in the title tag and description tag. The description tag should make sense and entice users to visit your site when they view the description on a search engine.

Your keywords should also be used in your H1 tag.

Use your keywords within the anchor text of the links. Assuming your best keyword phrase is "satellite affiliate", you should link to your home page using that keyword phrase. A good link to your home page might therefore look something like "satellite affiliate tips". Apply this linking method to all of the pages within your site. Furthermore, request that other sites link to you by using a similar anchor text containing your best keywords.

Keywords are one of the primary components in search engine optimization. They are the means by which search engines identify relevant pages for given searches. Using keywords effectively is one of the keys to achieving maximum traffic from the search engines.

BackLinks

Backlinks are a highly important and necessary part of any successful website. They are essential for Search Engine Optimization because they help to judge the popularity and importance of the website based on its links to other sites. Backlinks are actually rated by the various search engines by keywords and the content of the backlinked sites.

For example, if your site is about how to cook a hamburger, you would do better by linking to a site about recipes or food preparation than by linking to a site about downhill skiing. Why? Because search engines actually cross check the content of not only the link, but the actual sites the link is connecting, so they (search engines) can make sure the webmaster is not trying to gain higher SEO by doing things like running several unrelated sites at the same time and linking them together, using hidden links, or using automatically generated pages.

Backlinking is an effective way to generate website visits, but you have to understand that your site will not become popular overnight. Backlinking is a way of getting that needed traffic to your site and you have to do it correctly and smartly.

A great way to achieve visits is by linking other similar or related sites to yours. For instance, let's use the hamburger example again. That site should link to sites for frying pans, barbeques, or even sites that are associated with raising the cows. By doing this, the search engines will recognize that you are using quality links that fit into the area of your site's expertise.

Another way to create strong backlinks is through hyperlinks. When creating your hyperlinks, don't simply put "Click Here". Use "Visit the tips page for hints on how to make the best hamburger." This will ensure your links are using the same terms as your site and those you backlink to.

Part 5

Text Blog

—

No, It's Not An Online Diary

Text Blog—The Key To Providing Good Content

Blogs and websites that have rich content are always going to be more popular than those that don't. You may have wondered where these bloggers get their ideas, views and opinions. It's easy to write about something you're passionate about, but to do that several days a week is extremely hard. You'll either run out of things to talk about or you simply won't have the time.

So how do they do it? Where do they get their ideas? Do they get help from tools and other sources available on the Internet?

The very best way to fill your blog is to provide the content yourself. This is of utmost importance if your goal is to try to create traffic to an affiliated link. You'll definitely want to sell your site visitor on the importance of the services and products you're offering. That will set the stage or the "mood" and give authenticity to your affiliate link recommendations.

Expounding on the uses of a particular service or product, along with your own likes and dislikes, achieves this naturally. For an affiliate program, it's helpful if you have a personal anecdote that goes hand in hand with the product or service.

One way to find fresh ideas is to look for an appealing news article and then do a summary write-up based on it. It's not as easy as it sounds, but you and your readers will find it rewarding. If you feel that you just don't cut it as a writer or you genuinely don't have the time, then hire someone else to do it for you. Services like Elance.com, Odesk.com and Guru.com are just a few of the many services available to provide a "blog service" which includes daily posts of unique, engaging content. You can even instruct these content writers about where you want to point the links in your blog. This helps ease the burden of cost in terms of hiring them. The expense will be offset by the gains in your increased visitor base, the marketing of your other websites, and earnings from your affiliate programs.

Using private label articles is a viable alternative. PL articles abound on the Internet and you can always buy some that are connected to your central topic and then place them in your blog. One way of maximizing a purchased PL article is to cut it down into several pieces, thereby spreading its content over several postings.

Utilizing RSS feeds to post on blogs is becoming a popular choice. The advantage of an RSS feed is that your blog is automatically updated with fresh news and content from other websites. The disadvantage is that it is not unique content. Anyone interested will likely click on a story that appeals to them, and that click will cause them to leave your website.

These are the best ways to generate content for your blog. It is not advisable to use automated writing software. Those programs will give you plenty of content, but the substance of the text is unlikely to increase traffic for you. Putting in some good old-fashioned content work will always give you better results.

Part 6

Video Blog

—

Creating Great Relationships

Video Blog—The Key To Creating Great Relationships

Online video publishing has taken the Internet by storm in recent years. As a result, video is now being used for marketing, promotions, news and public relations. For internet marketers this has become a key strategic component and a business differentiator. Studies have shown that the average time a web user will stay on your site is 8 seconds. If you want to communicate effectively about your product, and profile it's benefits in the shortest possible time, you need to use video.

When web users search for information in a search engine, they will get thousands of search results. When they visit your website, they may only spend a few seconds and little effort to scan through what you are selling, and decide whether your content, style, look and approach are a good fit for what they were actually looking for. These first few seconds are crucial, and if you can deliver a clear and targeted message by offering a fast, highly visual way to get their further attention and engage their interest, you're website will have better results.

Does this mean that you just need to add a 10-minute video tutorial on your website? Unfortunately it's not that easy. (Is it ever?) Nor will you instantly sell more products and services just by plopping some randomly interesting video onto your page.

There are, however, some ways to make your video a good marketing tool. When done correctly a video can convey key traits and characteristics in a very short amount of time. And your customer will see your product in a unique, memorable way.

Get Your Video Seen

If you want your video to be an effective marketing tool, it must be seen by as many web users as possible. If you try to keep the video tight inside your website you'll be missing a lot of free traffic. Let your video content be freely distributed to the major sharing websites such as YouTube and Google Video. This will allow others to watch it and talk about it, plus they can easily download it, redistribute it, and even publish it directly to their own sites.

Small File & Fast Load

Statistics show that an average web user will only wait about 7 seconds for a page to load. For this reason you need to make sure your video file is small enough to load very quickly. Ideally it should be less than 1 MB to get the interest of your visitors before they click away. AVI is the most common video format for a camcorder, and the file size can easily reach 10 MB for a short 2-3 minute segment. Use a video format conversion program to convert it to mp3 or mpeg4. No need to look for anything fancy for this—your computer probably has one. Use Windows Movie Maker on a PC or iMovie on a Mac.

To Control, or Not to Control

When adding a video to your own website you can use a program that will take away all the control buttons. This keeps your site visitor from being able to fast forward, pause or stop the show. In addition, they can't see how long it is. Some marketers think this is useful, especially on a sales page, because the visitor is temporarily held captive. I personally find this very annoying, and will usually click away from the site.

I admit that I don't have much patience on a website. You might want to test it for a while both ways to see which style works best for your target customer.

Let Them Get To Know You

It's very, very effective to let your customers see you, hear you, and get to know you. I know this might be scary for you. It was scary for me for a long time. But it really works. Once you've allowed your followers to get to know the real you, they'll trust you and follow your recommendations without hesitation.

Part 7

The Squeeze Page

—

Capturing Names and Emails

Getting Your Readers To Take Action

In the world of Internet Marketing, the subscriber/ email list is considered the most important part of the business and even more important than the sale itself. That's because a good list will give you negotiating power for joint ventures or affiliate deals. As a result, marketers dedicate a large amount of time and money to collect a "list" of highly targeted subscribers.

Building a highly targeted subscriber list is probably the most profitable thing you can do on the internet. A highly targeted list of email subscribers will allow the owner to market either his product and service or other people's products with a fairly high degree of success. However, with the proliferation of spam, consumers are very careful about giving out their email addresses.

The best way to get people to subscribe to your list is to build a Squeeze Page (also called a landing page). A squeeze page is a simple page that has a headline, some text or video, and allows the visitor to register their name and email address in the field provided. A Squeeze Page can also be used as a tool to ease consumer concerns. Experienced online businesses create Squeeze Pages that detail what the subscriber will be receiving and the businesses privacy standards.

A Squeeze Page is not purely a web page with a capture form. It's main purpose is to generate leads by enticing visitors to give you their name and email address by offering something of value to them for free. Squeeze Pages should be designed in a way that draws the visitor's focus and attention to one thing, and that one thing is to take action by opting in to your list for more information. As a general rule, Internet Marketers try to keep the content on their Squeeze Pages to a minimum. There should be no links to other pages, or anything to distract the site visitor or cause them to navigate away to a different website.

The headline on your Squeeze Page is vitally important because it's the first contact point with your website's visitors. This is where you must captivate them by using an attention grabbing headline that compels them to take action. Your headline must be clear about what you are presenting, and your copy must connect with your visitors on an emotional level. Using a short video will also greatly increase the odds of people giving you their information.

A successful Squeeze Page has been known to have conversion rates of 30-60% and some even higher. The conversion rates mentioned here are the percentages of visitors that choose to opt-in to a mailing list by filling in the form fields available.

Squeeze Pages are often used in conjunction with an email auto-responder to begin delivering information as soon as the visitor confirms their email address. The auto-responder may be utilized to send a series of follow up emails or to provide an immediate download link to get information.

A proven effective method for increasing opt-ins is to promise your visitor some compelling information when they have entered and confirmed their email address. For example, if your mailing list targets basketball, you can offer a free e-book about bas-ketball. Once your subscribers join your email list, you should deliver the e-book quickly so you gain credibility. This delivery should be set up in an automated system so you can get new opt-in names at any time.

As soon as the free gift is sent, you can then direct your new customer to your sales page for more information.

Part 8

The
Sales Page

—

Creating a
Page That Gets
Buyers

Increase Your On-Line Success

As an internet marketer, your most important business tool is your website. This is your real estate on the web, and you'll only have a few seconds to get your customer's attention. For this reason, you need to consider many details about the design. There a several things to keep in mind if you want to create a website that sells.

Keeping in mind the old idiom "First impression is the last impression", a visitor's first look at the website is important in determining whether or not a visitor will want to buy from you. A professional look with soothing aesthetics, properly organized, quick loading and easily navigable website is the most important tool of your business.

- Design should be such that your websites ranks very high in search engines. The main factors that determine this are META tags, Title, Image, Keywords, ALT tags and the overall design.

- Use effective sales copy. Your business is founded on the words you use in the sales copy.

- Always showcase your testimonials. You can include testimonials right into your sales copy, either in text form or with video.

- Provide complete contact details. This will show

your visitors that you are completely transparent. Include an email address or phone number for requesting information or support.

- To increase sales, provide a guarantee on the products and services you're offering. If it suits your portfolio, you could also offer a money-back guarantee.

A professionally designed website is one of the most important factors in determining your on-line business success. It's important to test different colors and styles to determine the most effective way to turn your visitor into a buyer.

Facts Tell, Stories Sell

When creating any sales copy, there are some basic ingredients that you can use to dramatically increase your chances of making sales online and offline.

It would be nice if everyone would believe that you have the best "gidget & widget" out there. It would be even nicer if they believed it just because you said so. But the harsh reality is that most people won't simply take your word for it.

You need to give your potential customer the kind of information that will help them choose your product. This is most easily done by using stories, rather than facts.

Here's an example of some sales copy to sell the service of creating a customized company logo.

Ex #1 (Facts Only)
Company Logo Design—You will get

- 5 concepts to choose from

- Unlimited Revisions to 1 concept

- CD Included (All images print ready)

- Satisfaction Guaranteed!

- All of this for $199.00 CLICK HERE

Sounds like a good service for the price, right? Now let's add a story to these facts... see which one you would make you want to purchase.

Ex #2 (Story + Facts)

"PERFECT, that's the only word I can use when describing this company's logo design service. They not only saved me a lot of time, but they also spent most of their time finding out what I wanted. In the end they provided EXACTLY the type of logo I was looking for. Thank you so much!!!!"

We are here to help you succeed and want to deliver what you're looking for, not just what our designers want to create. Get a custom logo with these extra features attached:

• 5 Concepts to choose from

• Unlimited Revisions to 1 concept

• CD Included

• YOUR SATISFACTION GUARANTEED!

Do you see the difference between the two? In example #1, I displayed all the features and the price. In the 2nd example, I didn't add the price. Even without the price, example #2 will bring in more sales than example #1, simply because of the personal sounding connection.

It's all about "Fear Of Loss".

Fear of loss is a powerful tool to use. Don't tell people what they need. Have them fear the fact that if they don't have it, nothing will work out for them. A good industry for this example is Health and Beauty products, and specifically the sale of make-up. This industry has used "fear of loss" to it's fullest. They consistently insert into young female minds the need to use the advertised products in hopes of achieving the beauty that's promised in the ad.

By simply inserting a testimonial, as shown in the logo design example #2, your visitors will be much more likely to believe that you do have the best widget out there.

Part of the problem with turning your initial contacts into buying customers is the missing personal connection. People are simply sitting at a computer desk browsing through the internet. There's no personal touch to searching for services, and in your visitor's mind, the internet's only duty is to bring them the information they're seeking.

Testimonials and utilizing that fear of loss helps you to create a sub-conscious emotion that triggers an attachment to your company's services. If you've accomplished this correctly, your visitor might go looking at another company for the same services but, they will likely have problems concentrating on anything else after seeing your website.

Studies show that 8 out of 10 people choose a company based on a gut feeling, not facts. This is a very high number to lose by simply failing to appeal to their feelings.

Most of the time your visitor isn't able to see an actual sample of your product. You may show them a book cover, but it's not the same as being able to leaf through it at the bookstore. By adding testimonials your giving them an ability to hear what others think about your work, even if they can't see if for themselves. This goes a long way toward alleviating the fear of loss.

If you were thinking of hiring a company to provide a service for you, such as custom website design, they might provide a sensory rich display showing samples of their work. What would you feel like if you saw a portfolio that was full of great sites that not only looked good but also functioned perfectly? Would you feel excited to talk to these people at that affordable price? I know I would. On the other hand, if the price is right but the quality is poor, most of us will simply move onto the next web design company.

The more you can grab someone's attention and keep them interested online, the more they will learn to like you, trust you, and call you for your services, no matter the price.

Learn To Write Better Headlines

Headlines are the most important part of your sales letter. They account for 90% of your success. In other words, if you don't get your headlines right, your site won't sell.

The purpose of your headline is to get your site visitor excited. The goal is to grab your reader's attention and to make them continue reading your sales letter. If your headline fails to create excitement, it's very likely that your visitor will leave your site immediately and probably never return again.

How do you create excitement? You have to intrigue your readers with the fantastic benefits of your product. The headline of your sales letter has to present the most important benefit—the USP (Unique Selling Proposition) of your product.

Your headline should stir emotions and help your readers to imagine enjoying all the great benefits of your product. People buy for emotional reasons and that's why it's so important to describe the benefits of your product and not its features. Adding proven results will increase your success even further.

Your site visitors have only one question on their minds: What's in it for me? They're trying to figure out how to solve their problem, make more money, get the best job, look younger, etc. If you put your focus only on answering your customer's burning questions immediately, you'll write a great headline.

In your headline, tell your customers that you have a solution for their problem, that you have the answers to their questions, or that you will provide what they want.

As a result, your readers will be excited Immediately. They will be eager to continue reading through your sales letter, and chances are really good that you will get them to click on the "Buy Now" button at the end of your sales letter.

With practice you will learn how to write a great headline and getting the sale will become easy. Outstanding headlines can increase your sales by several hundred percent.

One headline isn't enough—use also subheadings
At the beginning of your sales letter you need to use your USP—the most compelling benefit of your product. Then, to keep your readers interested and excited, use several subheadings throughout your sales copy.

Each of these subheadings should convey a single benefit. This technique will pull your readers through your sales letter, right to the "Buy Now" button. If you don't keep your readers interested you risk losing them. So keep talking about the product benefits. Also, it's absolutely ok to state the same benefit several times in different ways.

Most web surfers only scan the page. They don't read every single word, but they will read your headlines. Therefore you have to make sure that a visitor who reads only your headlines understands exactly what he will get out of your product.

Make your reader's job easy. Divide your text into small logical blocks and start each block with a headline. This sub-headline is like an ad for the text that follows. It needs to convince your visitor to keep on reading.

Writing Effective Headlines

With a little practice you can learn to right great headlines. Here are some important points to consider as you're learning.

Write down all the benefits of your product. What kind of problems does it solve? How will it make your customer happier, healthier, wealthier?

You might not be aware of all the benefits. Think outside the box and keep on looking for more benefits. If possible, get input from someone who is familiar with your product. The more benefits you can include, the more exciting your product will sound.

What is the USP (Unique Selling Proposition) of your product. What makes it stand out from the crowd? What makes it unique? Whatever it is, that's your most important benefit. That's the one that will differentiate your product from those of your competitors.

Use short, active verbs that arouse emotions and create images.

Write your headlines only for your target customer and don't wory if someone else doesn't like it.

Here are some powerful words you can use in your

headlines: How to, Free, Why, Who wants to know, and Finally. You can also ask an open-ended question, like this: "Why do so many people fail to attract more money?"

Don't use too much hype. What you're saying has to be believable.

Brainstorm 10-20 headlines.

Pretend you are your customer. Which headline would get you excited? Which one stirs your emotions? Pick your three favorites and keep on modifying and changing them until you are really happy.

Take a break and come back the following day with a fresh mind, then do a final edit if necessary.

Learning how to write a great headline takes time and effort, but its absolutely crucial if you want to succeed as an internet marketer. It's very possible that you'll spend the same amount of time on your headlines as the whole rest of your sales letter... and that's perfectly ok.

Logo, Banner & Graphic Design

Your corporate logo, banner ads, and other graphic design aspects are key parts to a marketing campaign. It's important for your corporate logo to be unique, recognizable, and to reflect your type of business. Your corporate logo will be representative of everything your company is, and will indicate your company by its presence on your website, business cards, letterheads, advertisements, promotional items, and even buildings and company vehicles or uniforms, if applicable to your company.

Corporate logos are separated into three groups—descriptive logos, abstract logos, and typographical logos. Descriptive logos are an image, web banner design or logo design that suggests the company name or line of work. Abstract logos have no clear association to the company and rely on uniqueness and exposure to link the company to the logo. Typographical logos are logos based specifically on the name of the company. These attempt to take a well-known name and add a graphical appeal.

When it's time for a logo design, you may consider hiring a specialized firm to draft logos for your company. Many firms exist, so choose one with many years of experience, at least a handful of actual designers, and one whose previous work is appealing to you. A good firm has the knowledge and experience to help your company represent itself well graphically.

Banner ads are some of the most common advertising that is readily available today. A banner ad is a small advertisement usually found at the top of the web page. Nearly all free domain providers and networking sites rely on banner ad sales to make their profit, and certain studies suggest that banner ads with good web banner design at these sites provide more than 60% of hits to business sites. The success of a banner ad campaign relies in part on appropriate placement of the banner ad, but even more important is the design. Banner ads are so prevalent that all but the most innovative and eye-catching go unnoticed. The message must be clear, concise, professional, and backed up by eye-catching graphic design.

A few types of graphic designs have become available recently that come with a web2.0 look and feel which is very neat and clean. One style is a simple graphic design without any heavy colors, in gradients that just use simple, single colors. Another style uses 3D graphic design. These use heavy colors with reflections, and other techniques to make a more 3D look.

Once your banner ads have attracted potential customers to your web page, the site must continue to hold their attention. The site must be professional, informative, and easy to navigate, but must also have an appropriate graphical scheme. Your specific type of business and the image you want to portray will determine what type of graphical display you need for a logo design. Regardless of the feel that you desire for your website, it remains most important that the look be unique and appealing. Every page must be eye-catching, while having a theme and feel that will compliment your business. It should be appealing to the kind of person who will most likely be a potential customer for your business. When you have a graphic design that compliments your business, ties into your logo, and is part of a website that is easy to navigate, you will find an increase in sales, and greater success as a business.

Elements and Principles
of Graphic Design

Graphic design is actually the art and process of combining text and graphics to communicate an effective language in the design of logos, brochures, newsletters, posters and in fact, any type of visual communication. This is achieved by using several elements and design principles.

Always keep the design and layout of the graphic design as simple and clean as possible. Too much clutter makes it more difficult for the customer to find the important stuff! The color in your graphic design should be the same as your corporate colors. This will present consistency in all your advertising media, and people will subconsciously know how consistent you actually are! Never use all the colors of the rainbow in one design, as this only confuses the customer. Two or three colors from your corporate colors should be enough for your design.

There are tons of free fonts to be found on the internet, and these can be incorporated into your graphic design. Use a single font for the content of your design, and if required, you could use a different one, like a bolder and louder font, for the headings and titles of your graphic design. Using too many fonts only makes the graphic design look messy, and proves to confuse the audience. It is always beneficial to use images in the design of your brochures, company profiles, menus, etc. This way, you can entice your customers by illustrating your points through the images.

In graphic designing, it's important to use contrasting colors for the background and the font. If the font is a dark color, then a lighter colored background is preferred. While creating your graphic design, it's vital to stand back every once in a while to squint at your creation. Then notice the line of text and images in the graphic design. They should actually direct your customer's attention from the top of the page to the bottom, all in a seamless movement. If the line seems to be out of place, rearrange things to get a straight line.

When planning your graphic design, be aware of the traditional form of eye movement. We tend to automatically glance from top left to top right (probably because that's how we're taught to read). After that our eye makes a diagonal line to the bottom left, finally ending up in the bottom right. This is great for advertisements using lots of graphics or images. Always keep some white or empty space in the layout to give some rest to the eyes and some clarity to the existing information.

Maintain readability. A good presentation depends on the consistency of the ideas given. A well expressed design should not puzzle the customers mind, but rather make them understand what is being presented. Having readable text content will entice more visitors to want what you're offering.

Keep your design visually organized. The image, designs and illustrations used must be appropriate to your purpose and target audience. The designs applied should be based on the specifications given by you. Mainly, with the aid of a good graphic designer, you will be able to achieve the desired look for your material.

Keep your design relevant to your products or services. This will make your web site more popular and visitor friendly.

With the stiff competition in the present industry, gaining recognition is somewhat hard to attain. For you to be known and stand out among your competitors you must come up with an excellent design as well as informative content. With a little practice (or maybe some expert help), you will be able to achieve both.

Part 9

It's Payday!

The In's and Outs of Merchant Accounts

Choosing the Right Merchant Account Provider

As a business owner, you want to succeed. You undoubtedly want to increase your sales and make more money. The best way to do this is to offer your customers the ability to pay for merchandise with their credit cards. Whether you operate your business in a physical location or online only, allowing customers the option of credit card payment is logical. You will increase sales because of the convenience of the payment options you offer. The vast majority of shoppers, online and in person, prefer to pay with their credit cards. Opening a merchant account is the way to give your customers more payment options. For this reason it's important that you find out as much as you can about merchant accounts and merchant account providers.

A merchant account is set up through a bank or an online merchant account provider for a retail or online organization in order to accept credit cards as payment from customers. A merchant account is not a bank account. The merchant account provider's job is to place the money you earn from credit card sales into your bank account. It used to be that merchant accounts were only offered by banks and providers to retail businesses that were located in a physical location. But with online shopping gaining popularity over the past several years, merchant account providers have started providing accounts to online business owners as well. Even though most banks still do not provide online merchant accounts due to the constant concern over credit card fraud, there are an increasing number of online merchant account providers who offer services specifically to those merchants that market their products online. Because of the high number of merchant account providers out there, it's important that you research all aspects of them, what services they provide, and especially the costs they impose, so you don't lose precious profits.

When looking into merchant accounts and providers, be aware that there are two types of payment processing they'll offer. One is manual and the other is "real time" processing. Manual processing requires that the credit card number be delivered through a phone transaction, fax transaction, or an online order form. The order is processed manually by contacting the payment processing company (usually through an Internet connection) to verify the credit card number, or by using a point of sale machine to swipe the card at the time of purchase. This type of processing is more secure, less costly, and ideal for a low-volume merchant in a physical store location. Real-time processing is perfect for web-based merchants because the credit card is immediately processed at the time an order is placed. Pending verification and approval of the credit card, the customer receives notification (via e-mail) that his or her order is accepted and fund transfer is approved.

This is the less secure of the two processing options.

There are costs associated with opening and sustaining a merchant account. Not all of the fees are necessary, and not all merchant account providers will charge them. One type of cost is the application fee, which covers the costs of processing your application, whether you open an account or not. A number of merchant account providers will waive the fee if you decide to open an account. Some merchant account providers don't charge this fee at all. There's often an annual fee associated with a merchant account as well. Merchant account providers charge this fee simply for holding an account with them. Another common fee is the statement fee, a monthly fee that can be as much as $25 per month, and is supposedly imposed by the account providers in order to cover their own costs. Yet another fee is the discount rate, which the merchant account provider earns from each of your sales, usually between 2 and 4 percent. The fixed transaction fee, like the discount fee, is also based on each sale, but the provider takes the same amount regardless of the cost of the product purchased, usually .20-.30. Usually, buried in the fine print of your agreement with your provider is a termination fee. Because some providers require a lengthy commitment period of more than 2 years, this fee applies if you cancel your account early.

There are also various miscellaneous fees that are

levied on your account. Often, these charges are withdrawn if a customer requests a refund, and wants the amount credited back to their card. Because there are many costs associated with an online merchant account, it can cut into your profits. It's important that you evaluate different merchant account providers you're interested in, so you can save yourself money down the line. You can also use your current sales information to guesstimate the costs of your merchant account.

It's likely you'll have a long relationship with your merchant account provider. Therefore, you should have the utmost trust and confidence in them. Your provider should offer various services that will give you options in making your business transactions run smoothly. They should be able to accommodate several brands of credit cards (Visa, Mastercard, Discover, American Express, etc.), in addition to providing other payment alternatives, such as PayPal. They should have a record of impeccable service and reliability. They should also be first-rate customer service providers. Any problems should be handled discreetly and quickly. Despite the seeming necessity of having a merchant account provider, it can make or break your business with its fees and service. Choose carefully and the benefits will outweigh the costs.

Accepting Credit Cards Without a Merchant Account

Sometimes using the services of a credit card processor is a better option, at least when starting out if you haven't already established a merchant account. In this way, you may process credit card transactions without the high front-end costs and requirements of a merchant account.

Here, then, are just a few ways of accepting credit cards without a merchant account.

Clickbank

If your product is downloadable (such as electronic books or software), you might consider ClickBank. com. For a $49.95 initial fee, you can process credit cards and on-line checks. Your only fees will be $1.00 per transaction plus 7.5% of sales.

You receive additional exposure through free listing on their website and through the search facilities of other websites, such as CBMall.com.

As an added bonus, you'll have your own built-in affiliate program. You decide what commission (from 1% to 75%) you would like to pay your affiliates.

PayPal

PayPal.com has no initial fees. For just 2.9% of sales and $ .30 per transaction (and sometimes less), you can receive money from anyone.

Also, this service allows you to pay others by credit card or checking account without supplying your personal credit information to the payee. PayPal can be used to collect money from your auctions, web-site sales, or even from friends or clients.

PaySystems

"PaySystems.com can handle either intangible (down-loadable) or tangible (shippable) products. For an initial fee of $49.00, you can accept all major credit cards as well as online checks. Fees are just 3.95% of sales and $1.00 per transaction. They offer an alternative choice in which you may pay 5.5% of sales and $ .35 per transaction. For this you receive a shopping cart, integration with third-party affiliate programs, fraud screening, multi-currency transactions, toll-free support, marketing tools, and more. Unfortunately, PaySystems.com has discontinued their "Internet Billing Account" for those outside the United States.

2CheckOut

2CheckOut.com can handle both intangible and tangible products. For an initial fee of $49.00, you can accept all major credit cards as well as online checks. Fees are just 5.5% of sales and $0.45 per transaction. Your account includes a shopping cart, fraud detection, integration with third-party affiliate programs, multi-currency transactions, free on-line support, and more.

Incidentally, 2CheckOut.com has the same policy as ClickBank.com with regard to sales taxes. Both companies take the position that you are selling your product to them and that they resell it to the final consumer. Thus, they claim that you are not subject to sales taxes on those sales.

Part 10

Customer Service Counts

Creating a New Standard of Excellence

Many of our customer service experiences over the years have significantly lowered our expectations. If you're like me, I'm sure you've had times when it took days (or even weeks) to get an appointment with someone to fix a broken appliance, get a health check-up or repair your computer. You may have also experienced rude employees, either in person or over the phone.

The good news is that by providing an excellent customer service experience, it's easier than ever to really stand out. When you are good, people notice. When you are excellent, they rave.

This is true for us personally, professionally, or as an organization.

Below are some steps you can take to continue to raise your own standards of excellence. These steps will make it easier than ever to stand out, be noticed, and have greater levels of success and satisfaction.

Get a Current Reading on Performance

Talk to those you've served, whether online or off. Find out from them how well you're currently doing in meeting their expectations. Listen to their feedback. Don't justify your current performance or blame others. Just listen.

Determine the Standard They Want
Make notes of their needs, wants and hopes.

Determine the Standard You Want
Remember that their expectations may not be very high, based on their previous experiences. Take their feedback and ideas into account, but remember that it is your responsibility to set the level of excellence you want to reach. Set the bar as high as you wish.

Under Promise and Over Deliver
Taking the first three steps will heighten your awareness and likely raise your own expectations immediately. As you work to grow your standards remember that you can reach your goal in small steps. Make promises based on your current capability, not your fondest wish. Make the promise, then deliver more, then raise the level of your promise a bit more the next time. Slow and steady wins the race—and remember it won't take long to leave those you are racing with far behind. This approach will help you raise your standards, and others will automatically start to trust you more.

Ask "What's Not Excellent?"
By asking this question you will continue to find ways to improve your standards and delivery. Ask this question of yourself, of your teammates, and of other interested parties.

Customer Service is Now Customer Care

As I waited on hold for an answer to an appliance issue I had, the recording stated that a "customer care" representative would be available shortly. At that moment I realized it's finally catching on everywhere. With aging baby boomers, world events and additional pressures in today's society, it is "customer care" that has evolved in our economy. We have moved from a manufacturing economy to a service economy and are currently leaning toward a "service care" economy. As we live in a high tech, button touch environment, many personal contacts have been decreased, making each customer interaction more important than ever to your company's image. For example, if you call for computer tech support, the representative often makes it a point to address you by first name. If it's the bank credit card company, they may ask "How are you doing today?" Their hope is that this makes you feel less like a number and more like a human being.

A recent survey asked diners why they went out to eat and the main response was "to feel good." (After all, the word "restaurant" has French origins meaning "to restore"). As a waitress for many years, I felt my job was to restore humanity, especially to diners arriving from a stressed out day.

In my past dining room work experiences, I remember

certain actions that lifted service to this higher level of "care." One time a customer requested margarine that wasn't available in the restaurant. The owner walked across the street to the grocery store, purchased the margarine and delivered it to the table. The customer was delighted. There was a regular customer (diabetic) who always got immediate attention with some kind of bread or crackers to keep from feeling faint before her food arrived. If there was a baby present at a table, our staff ensured their food would come out as soon as possible to pacify. These kinds of actions create a lasting positive image for any company or establishment. The owner cared about his guests and it permeated throughout the dining room and to the staff.

Customer Service involves major 3 points:

1. Care and Concern for the Customer

2. Spontaneity and Flexibility of frontline workers, which enhances the ability for on-the-spot problem-solving

3. Recovery—making things right with the customer when something has gone wrong

These 3 points should always be highlighted in any customer service training program. If you keep them in mind, you will be known for the quality service you deliver.

Customer Service Tips
That Generate Referrals

To achieve the "wow" factor in your customer's experience, you must be honest, knowledgeable, friendly, professional and deliver on your promises. In addition, you must be able to provide a high level of service to everyone who comes in contact with your business. If you do, you'll also get more referrals from your satisfied clients.

Apply the "wow" to everyone who comes in contact with you and your business. Good service means you want people to be blown away by the extraordinary level of care you deliver to your clients. Demonstrate your exceptional level of customer service by showing your generosity through gift giving. Your goal should be to deliver such a high level of service that your clients can't wait to tell their family members, friends and co-workers about your company.

Everyone who comes into contact with your business is a potential client or referrer. Look for a reason to send your customers a thank you card along with a gift.

So, what types of gifts should you send? I'll leave that up to your imagination, but here are some relatively inexpensive ideas to help you get started:

- Movie passes

- Starbucks cards

- Flowers, houseplants

- A ticket for a free car wash

- Gift candles

- Favorite recipes

- Gourmet chocolates or gourmet popcorn

Successful sales people always make sure their faithful referrers are regularly and consistently rewarded. Set aside the best rewards for your top referrers. This may include:

- Dinner for two at a fancy restaurant

- Tickets to the opera or to a rock concert

- A gift card

- High end fruit or gift basket

- Potted plant or flower arrangement

- A personally inscribed pen

When it comes to gift giving the sky is the limit. The more personal the gift, the more likely it will be remembered and it will serve as a thoughtful reminder to your best referrers the next time some- one is in need of your exemplary services.

Delivering Great Customer Service

It almost goes without saying that good customer service is essential to sustaining any business. No matter how wonderful a job you do of attracting new customers, you won't be profitable for long unless you have a solid customer retention strategy in place—and in action. It's the actions that count—not what you say you'll do, or what the policy says. People will remember what you or your employees have done—or not done.

One of the key components of an effective retention strategy is exceptional customer service. Not just good service, but memorable service. Today, consumers' expectations are higher than ever and companies that fail to deliver risk losing market share.

Here are some things you can do:

Personalize Each Experience

One of the best examples I've ever seen of this is at my local coffee shop. One day I noticed that the young man behind the counter greeted some people by name and, even if he didn't know their name, he knew what they usually ordered. As I waited for my tea, I asked him why he said, "See you later" to some customers, "See you tomorrow" to others, yet always said, "Have a good week" to me. The smiling, friendly reply? "Because you only come in on Mondays and Fridays." He really paid attention to his regular customers and personalized their experience.

Be Polite!
Too frequently company representatives ask customers for information without saying "Please" or even being polite. A survey conducted by Schulich School of Business MBAs suggests that this kind of problem exists in over 30% of companies, and costs them hundreds of millions of dollars in lost customers (and revenues) each and every year. Don't let your company end up one of these statistics.

Thank Your Customers
Too often, customers receive a rushed and barely civil "Thanks-have-a-nice-day" and the sales clerk is off to the next customer. With large purchases, a verbal greeting should be followed up with a hand-written card, not just because it leads to increased referrals (which is does), but because it will leave a positive, lasting impression on your customer.

Appearances Do Count!
According to two independent pieces of research, nearly 90% of customers form an impression about how competent and reputable your company is based on what they see when they first walk through your doors or visit your website.

Be Real and Respond Quickly
People want to connect with human beings. Give them quick and easy ways to connect with you

through email, a Contact Us section on your website or a phone number where you can be reached during specified hours. As your company grows, consider adding a live chat to your website with 24/7 service.

Do What You Say You Will...
When You Say You Will

One of the quickest ways to lose customer confidence is to not follow-through, or to be late delivering a service or product, without notifying the customer in advance, determining whether or not the delay will impact the customer and providing an alternate solution in the interim if necessary.

Surprise the Customer From Time To Time

When it's possible to provide an extra level of service, do so. Whether it's an unexpected complimentary dessert in a restaurant, or an upgrade that has not been requested, these special gestures go a long way toward building customer loyalty.

Provide "Full" Service

When you order a pair of shoes from Zappos, they pay for the shipping to get them to you and they also pay the shipping on any returns. That's full service! And it has contributed greatly to their overwhelming success. Small things, yes. Greatly appreciated? No question. In speaking with some of my local retailers, I learned that in each case, their sales—and profits—have enjoyed double digit increases since they introduced more comprehensive service. One woman I know who owns a toy store started offering "curbside service" as well as gift wrapping. When a customer knows what they want and are in a hurry (getting their child to a birthday party without time to shop), they just call up, order, and the gift is wrapped and ready at a specific time and is brought to their car when they pull up to the store. That's another example of "Full Service" that goes beyond the ordinary. Think about what you can add to help make things easier for your customers. In some cases, by looking at what else it makes sense to sell, you can even add a new revenue stream while improving the perceived level of customer service provided.

Mea Culpa

When you have made a mistake, admit it and set things straight. When customers have a complaint—listen, truly listen. Then apologize and take corrective action. In many instances, the very act of listening (without interrupting) can be enough to diffuse the situation and make the person feel worthy as a customer. Then ask the customer how they would like you to resolve the situation. In most cases your client will come up with something reasonable—and often less costly than a solution you might have proposed.

Listen To Your Customers

Conduct your own surveys and get feedback on what they like and don't like—and take corrective action as required. Let customers know that their business is appreciated and that their opinions are important to you.

None of these suggestions takes a lot of time or money to implement, yet they can pay dividends in increased customer relationships and retention.

About the Author

In 1997 Bonnie Dye left the corporate rat race to become an entrepreneur. She now owns and manages several small businesses, where every day brings something new and exciting.

As an experienced facilitator, author and internet marketing strategist, Bonnie enjoys coaching individuals to help them grow their companies. She currently leads a monthly mastermind group of small business owners and conducts weekly training sessions to help people increase their online presence.

www.ingramcontent.com/pod-product-compliance
Lightning Source LLC
Chambersburg PA
CBHW071221050326
40689CB00011B/2403